SICILY TRAVEL GUIDE 2023

"Unveiling the Treasures of Sicily: Your Ultimate Travel Companion for 2023"

Gloria E. Freeman

Copyright©2023 by *Gloria E. Freeman*

Allrightsreserved.No part of this publication may be reproduced, stored or transmitted in any form or by any means, electronic, mechanical, photocopying, recording, scanning, or otherwise without written permission from the publisher. It is illegal to copy this book, post it to a website, or distribute it by any other means without permission. *Gloria E. Freeman* asserts the moral right to be identified as the author of this work.

TABLE OF CONTENT

INTRODUCTION TO SICILY
- Brief Overview of the Island
- Historical Significance and Cultural Diversity
- Why Visit Sicily in 2023?

CHAPTER 1 PLANING YOUR TRIP
- Best Time to Visit
- Visa and Entry Requirements
- Budgeting & Currency
- Transportation Options

CHAPTER 2 EXPLORING TOP DESTINATION
- Palermo: Capital City and Cultural Hub
- Taormina: Coastal Beauty and Ancient Ruins

- Catania: Vibrant Markets and Mt. Etna Views
- Agrigento: valley of the temples
- Syracuse: Ancient Greek and Roman Treasures

CHAPTER 3 NATURAL WONDERS

- Mount Etna: Europe's Tallest Active Volcano
- Aeolian Islands: Unspoiled Paradise
- Zingaro Nature Reserve: Coastal Hiking and Scenery

CHAPTER 4 IMMERSIVE CULTURAL EXPERIENCES

- Local Festivals and Celebrations
- Traditional Cuisine and Local Delicacies
- Sicilian Wines and Vineyards

CHAPTER 5 HISTORICAL SITES AND ARCHITECTURE

- Norman Cathedrals and Arab-Norman Palaces
- Segesta: Ancient Temple and Theater
- Selinunte: Greek Ruins by the Sea

CHAPTER 6 OUTDOOR ACTIVITIES

- Beaches and Water SportsHiking and Trekking Routes

CHAPTER 7 PRACTICAL TIPS FOR TRAVELERS

- Language and Communication
- Safety and Health Considerations
- Locals Etiquette and Customs

CHAPTER 8 RECOMMENDED ITINERARIES

- 5-Day Cultural Exploration
- 7-Day Adventure and Nature Tour
- 10-Day Grand Tour of Sicily

CHAPTER 9 USEFUL RESOURCES
ACCOMMODATION OPTIONS
- Tour Operators and Guides

CHAPTER 10: PACKING LIST, MONEY SAVING IDEAS AND ITALIAN LOCAL PHRASES.
- Packing List
- Budgeting techniques
- Italian Local Phrase
  Conclusion

INTRODUCTION TO SICILY

Sicily is the largest island in the Mediterranean Sea. It is a fascinating place with a varied culture, rich history, breathtaking landscapes, and influences from many other civilizations. Nestled at the meeting point of Europe and Africa, this Italian island has long been a melting pot of civilizations, influencing its architecture, food, and overall way of life.

Sicily's history extends back thousands of years, during which time it was inhabited by many groups of people including the Greeks, Romans, Byzantines, Arabs, Normans, and Spanish. A distinctive fusion of architectural styles and customs has resulted from the imprints left by various civilizations on the island. Many historical sites may be found throughout the island, including the breathtaking archaeological site known as the Valley of the Temples in Agrigento.

Brief Overview of the Island

The largest island in the Mediterranean, Sicily is a fascinating travel destination known for its fascinating history, varied culture, and breathtaking scenery. Sicily has a long history and has been affected by many different civilizations over the years, such as the Greeks, Romans, Arabs, Normans, and Spanish. This has led to a distinctive fusion of architectural styles and customs. The island's varied cultures are reflected in its food, which features ingredients like fresh fish, veggies grown nearby, and fragrant herbs. Sicily's diverse landscapes, which range from golden beaches to towering mountains, including the famous Mount Etna, showcase the island's natural splendor. The island is a captivating and engaging tourist destination because of its festivals and customs, which highlight its rich culture even more.

Historical Significance and Cultural Diversity

Tucked down in the center of the Mediterranean, Sicily is a living example of how history and culture have interwoven to create its intricate fabric. With a rich cultural legacy reflecting the many civilizations that have left their lasting imprints on its shores, this charming Italian island has a millennium-long history.

A patchwork of influences from the many ancient civilizations that have called Sicily home have shaped the island's historical significance. In the eighth century BC, the

Greeks founded colonies here, and the Valley of the Temples is a testament to their architectural and cultural legacy. The exceptionally well-preserved Greek temples within this archaeological marvel attest to the island's significance as a crossroads of cultures.

The history of Sicily also included Roman domination, which left remarkable ruins such as the Roman Villa del Casale, renowned for its elaborate mosaics depicting stories of everyday life in that era. Cities such as Palermo and Syracuse have an intriguing fusion of architectural forms, influenced by the influences of the Byzantines, Arabs, Normans, and Spaniards.

Sicily's status as a melting pot of civilizations fosters cultural variety. Mirroring its history, the island's cuisine is a delicious blend of tastes. While couscous dishes highlight the island's ties to North Africa, meals like arancini, rice balls packed with ragù and cheese, pay homage to Arab influences. Culinary skill refined over ages is exemplified by the famous Sicilian cannoli, a pastry shell filled with creamy ricotta.

The island's many cultural influences are on display during religious festivals. Palermo's Feast of Santa Rosalia, which honors the patron saint with a magnificent procession, is a reflection of the city's deeply ingrained Catholic traditions. In contrast, the extravagant parades and feasts that accompany Catania's Festival of Saint Agatha honor the island's historical connections to Byzantium.

Language reflects the richness of Sicily's culture as well; the dialect spoken in Sicily is a blend of Arabic, Spanish, Italian, and other languages. The island's multiracial background and connectivity are captured in this linguistic fusion.

The historical significance and cultural richness that characterize Sicily would surely be highlighted in a trip guide published in 2023, to sum up. Sicily has assimilated and stitched together a complex web of customs, architecture, and gastronomy with each succeeding civilisation to grace her shores. Sicily's fascinating journey through time can be glimpsed through seeing its ancient ruins, indulging in its delicious cuisine, and attending its vibrant festivals. In addition to breathtaking scenery, this location provides a deep dive into the fabric of human history and cultural development.

Why Visit Sicily in 2023?

In 2023, there will be a wonderful opportunity to visit Sicily and fully immerse oneself in a captivating blend of historical wonders, cultural diversity, and natural beauty. Here are some compelling justifications for why now is the ideal time to travel to this lovely Italian island:

In 2023, during the Cultural Renaissance, Sicily's rich cultural heritage will be honored and protected. Numerous festivals, exhibitions, and events that let you engage closely with the island's past and present are likely to highlight the historical value of the place.

gastronomic treats Sicilian food, a feast for the senses, will allow you to experience the island's rich diversity of flavors in 2023. This is a chance to sample real Sicilian cuisine at its finest, with street markets selling fresh fish and trattorias serving mouthwatering dinners.

Reduced Crowding at Attractions: Compared to peak travel times, 2023 might offer a less crowded experience at popular tourist spots like the Valley of the Temples and Mount Etna. This enables you to visit historical sites and stunning natural settings more peacefully.

Examining Natural Beauty: Sicily is home to stunning landscapes, including hrilling festivals, this year offers a terrific opportunity to explore its attractions while enjoying a more true and immersive experience.

CHAPTER 1 Planning Your Trip

Best Time to Visit

The shoulder seasons of spring (April to June) and fall (September to October) are the ideal times to travel to Sicily, Italy. It is the perfect time to discover the island's rich history, breathtaking landscapes, and vibrant culture during these months because of the excellent weather and reduced crowds.

Mid-60tts to mid-70s Fahrenheit (18–24°C) are the typical springtime temperatures. Wildflowers in bloom and luxuriant vegetation give the island its vibrant hue. The weather is perfect for outdoor pursuits like hiking, sightseeing, and taking in the Mediterranean shoreline. The pleasant weather makes it comfortable to see well-known sights like Mount Etna, historic sites, and quaint seaside communities.

With temperatures in the mid-70s to the mid-80s Fahrenheit (24–30°C), autumn is just as pleasant. There is now less of a summer crowd, making for a more calm experience. While grape harvesting is in full swing in the vineyards, the sea is still warm, making swimming and other water sports possible. Food festivals honoring regional cuisine and specialties are also popular at this time of year.

The summer months of July and August may be quite hot, with frequent highs of 90°F (32°C) drawing throngs of people. Despite how appealing the beaches are, the heat and packed attractions may make the trip less enjoyable altogether. Consider visiting coastal cities or islands with refreshing sea breezes if you're eager to travel throughout the summer.

Although the winter months of November to February can be very moderate, other regions may get rain and lower temperatures. The off-season is a fantastic time to explore indoor cultural events and savor Sicilian food.

In conclusion, spring and autumn are the greatest seasons to visit Sicily since they have warm temperatures, beautiful scenery, and manageable visitor crowds. Without the extremes of summer heat or winter cold, these seasons offer the perfect balance for taking part in outdoor activities, visiting historical sites, and appreciating the local culture.

Visa and Entry Requirements

The conditions for entering Sicily and Italy as of my most recent update in September 2021 vary on your country and the reason for your trip. It's crucial to remember that laws may have changed since then, so always double-check with official sources or the Italian embassy or consulate in your area before making travel arrangements.

For short stays (up to 90 days) for tourist, business, or family visits, most visitors—especially those from the European Union (EU) and Schengen Area countries—might not need a visa. Some non-EU nations, however, need their nationals to obtain a Schengen visa in order to enter Italy. Travel to and within the Schengen Area, which includes Italy, is permitted with this visa.

If your country doesn't require a visa for entry, you'll need:

an authentic passport Make sure your passport is valid for at least three months after the day you intend to leave the Schengen Zone.

Affirmation of accommodations: Have your hotel bookings or an Italian host's letter of invitation ready.

Proof of sufficient funds: You might be asked to provide evidence that you have enough cash on hand to cover your stay-related expenses.

Onward or return transportation: You must show proof that you intend to leave the Schengen Zone following your visit.

The best course of action is to purchase travel insurance that includes emergency medical coverage and medical expenses.

supplementary materials You could require other paperwork, such as a letter from your employment, an invitation for business, or documents pertaining to your family, depending on the reason for your visit.

You would need to apply for the proper visa from an Italian consulate or embassy before your trip if you were planning longer visits or other purposes, such as a job, study, or residency.

Recall that admittance requirements can alter, therefore it's essential to check with official sources for the most recent details. You should be able to find complete and accurate information on the visa and entrance criteria for your particular circumstances on the Italian government's official website or at the consulate in your country.

Budgeting & Currency

Accommodations, travel, food, activities, and any unforeseen costs should all be taken into account when creating a budget for a vacation to Sicily. Here are some general budgeting principles and details on the currency as of my most recent update in September 2021:

Accommodations: The cost of a hotel can vary significantly depending on its location, amenities, and season. Both upscale resorts and affordable options may be available. Especially during the busiest travel seasons, think about making reservations in advance.

Buses, trains, and ferries are just a few of the well-connected modes of transportation in Sicily. Transportation costs vary according to distance and mode of travel. Consider rental costs, fuel costs, tolls, and parking if you intend to rent a vehicle.

Dining expenses vary, although Sicily is renowned for its delectable.

Transportation Options

Sicily provides visitors with a wide range of means of transportation to get across the island's varied topography and discover its charming towns, important landmarks, and breathtaking coasts. You can choose from a variety of transportation options when visiting Sicily, each of which can be customized to your needs and financial situation.

1. **Public transportation:**

   Transport by train: Sicily has a robust rail system that connects its major cities and towns. With both regional and long-distance trains, Trenitalia manages the majority of train services. In order to get about the island, the trains offer a convenient and beautiful method of transportation.

Another popular form of public transit in Sicily is the bus. They provide service to both urban and rural areas, giving them an efficient option for moving about smaller towns and villages.

Sicily is an island, so ferries and hydrofoils are essential for getting there and moving throughout the island's many areas. Aeolian Islands, Sardinia, and Malta are just a few of the adjacent islands that Sicily is connected to along with the Italian mmainland.

2. Rental vehicles

Renting a Car: If you want to have more freedom and flexibility while traveling, renting a car is a great choice for seeing Sicily's more rural parts. Narrow streets and little parking, however, can make driving in some cities difficult. If your travels will take you outside of the main cities, think about renting a ccar.

3. **Using taxis and ridesharing**:

Taxis: Taxis are an easy method to get around, especially if you're pressed for time or traveling with a group. Taxis are readily available in most cities. In comparison to other modes of transportation, they can be somewhat more eexpensive.

4. **Ride-sharing**:

In some places, there exist ride-sharing services like Uber that provide an alternative to standard taxis

.

5. **Bicycles**:

Cycling can be a relaxing and environmentally beneficial way to discover new surroundings in some places. There are programs for renting bikes in some cities, and in some places, there may be designated cycling routes.

Wandering about Sicilian towns and cities on foot, especially in their ancient districts, can be a wonderful way to discover their beauty. You may easily negotiate narrow streets while walking and take in the atmosphere of the nneighborhood.

6. **Domestic flights**:

Domestic flights are a possibility if you wish to swiftly go farther distances, even though they are not usually necessary for navigating about the island. Palermo, Catania, and Trapani are home to Sicily's three primary airports.

There are benefits and things to keep in mind for each type of transportation in Sicily. Your decision will be influenced by a number of variables, including your itinerary, financial situation, level of comfort, and the places you intend to see. To get the most out of your Sicilian vacation, it is advised to arrange your transportation and do some study beforehand. If you want to travel, make sure to verify the most recent information because transportation alternatives and services might have changed since my September 2021 update.

CHAPTER 2 Exploring Top Destinations

Palermo: Capital City and Cultural Hub

Palermo, a city molded by history, culture, and civilization, is perched along the Mediterranean Sea's turquoise shore and serves as a monument to the passage of time. The lively tapestry of Palermo, the Italian region of Sicily's capital, combines a complex fusion of influences to form a cultural center that fascinates tourists with its diversity, architectural wonders, and historical significance.

As rich and intricate as its architecture is Palermo's history. It served as a hub for a number of civilizations, including the Phoenicians, Romans, Arabs, and Normans. Through its architecture, streets, and monuments, this mingling of civilizations is eloquently displayed. In addition to providing a window into the past, the cityscape serves as a living museum, displaying the interaction of various forces that have molded the city's character.

Nothing less than awe-inspiring can be said about the city's architectural gems. The Palermo Cathedral, a fusion of Gothic, Norman, and Arab styles, is a representation of Palermo's diversity in terms of architecture. Intricate mosaics from the Norman Palace's magnificent Palatine Chapel are on display, reflecting the city's multiethnic past. As places where vendors have been selling their items for decades, lively and bustling marketplaces like Ballar and Vucciria inspire a sense of timelessness.

Palermo is a vibrant, thriving center of culture; it is not merely a throwback to another era. A vibrant blend of tradition and contemporary can be seen in the city's cultural landscape. Palermo is a thriving center for artistic expression, hosting everything from art galleries and theaters to music festivals and contemporary exhibitions. World-class performances are presented at one of Europe's biggest opera houses, the Teatro Massimo, which draws guests from all over the world.

The cultural experience in Palermo is further enhanced by culinary delights. Greek, Arab, and Spanish traditions have all influenced Sicilian food, which itself is a reflection of the history of the area. Local fare such as arancini (rice balls), panelle (chickpea fritters), and cannoli (sweet pastries) tantalizes the palate and offers a gastronomic voyage through time.

The festivals and customs of Palermo reflect the city's cultural significance. Santa Rosalia is the patron saint of the city, and each year, hundreds of people flock there for the beautiful festival honoring her. The celebrations showcase the very essence of Palermo's cultural legacy through a fusion of religious fervor, folklore, and energetic parades.

Finally, Palermo captures the spirit of diversity and history as Sicily's capital and cultural center. Its stunningly blended architecture, which combines many different forms, depicts centuries of coexistence and adaptation. Drawing on both history and innovation, the cultural environment is thriving with inventiveness. A diverse tapestry of cultures that have coexisted and prospered within Palermo's boundaries adds to the city's allure in addition to its gorgeous landmarks and picturesque streets. Visits to Palermo are journeys across time as much as they are through the city.

Taormina: Coastal Beauty and Ancient Ruins.

Taormina is a stunning representation of ancient history and seaside beauty, located on Sicily's northeastern coast. This picturesque town is well known for its stunning views of the Mediterranean Sea, its quaint alleyways, and its well-preserved ancient remains that transport visitors to a bygone period.

Nothing short of enchanting describes Taormina's coastline allure. The village boasts expansive views of the Mediterranean's turquoise waves because it is perched high on a hill. The most active volcano in Europe, Mount Etna, rising in the distance, gives a dramatic touch to the already gorgeous environment. All who visit are left with an enduring impression of the turquoise sea colors contrasted with the luxuriant foliage.

The ancient ruins that dot the countryside around Taormina offer a peek into the past. The Greek Theatre, an engineering and architectural marvel from antiquity, is the most well-known of these. The theater, which was carved into the hillside, provides performances with an unmatched setting thanks to its breathtaking vistas of the sea and Mount Etna. The theater, which dates back to the third century BC, has long served as a forum for cultural enrichment. It has held innumerable theatrical productions and musical performances over the years.

The town itself is a labyrinth of winding streets and quaint lanes, offering a delightful fusion of neighborhood stores, cafes, and boutiques for artists. The distinctive fusion of Sicilian culture and history that permeates every nook can be experienced by tourists as they stroll through the streets. Taormina's main street, Corso Umberto, is a bustling promenade dotted with cute boutiques, tempting gelato stalls, and energetic cafes that together create a vibrant ambiance that is both active and soothing.

In addition to its historic ruins, Taormina is home to a vibrant cultural scene. The town holds a number of festivals and events all throughout the year, from local celebrations that capture the essence of Sicilian culture to classical music performances and film festivals. Visitors get the chance to become fully immersed in the local culture and build relationships with the locals thanks to these events.

Taormina's culinary treats are an accurate representation of the abundance of the area. A delicious variety of traditional Sicilian cuisine is available at nearby restaurants, with fresh seafood, ingredients that are found locally, and recipes that have been handed down through the years. Taormina dining is more than just a meal; it's a sensory excursion through the tastes and fragrances of Sicily.

The combination of Taormina's coastline beauty and historic history is what gives the city its charm, to sum up. Visitors will have an amazing experience because of its breathtaking scenery, well-preserved ruins, and dynamic cultural environment. Taormina offers a timeless getaway that mixes coastal views, old street exploration, and discovering the ruins of past civilizations.

Catania: Vibrant Markets and Mt. Etna Views

The city of Catania, which is located on Sicily's east coast, hums with lively marketplaces, old-world elegance, and Mount Etna's imposing presence. This bustling location provides visitors with a distinctive fusion of local culture, breathtaking scenery, and a lengthy history.

The crowded marketplaces in Catania are one of its most distinguishing characteristics. The city's outdoor markets, like the renowned "La Pescheria," radiate a vibrant energy that stimulates the senses. The heart of Sicilian culinary tradition is displayed through colorful displays of fresh vegetables, fragrant spices, and regional specialties. The markets offer a chance to see daily life in its fullness while shopping and mingling with sellers and residents.

The beautiful Mount Etna background that surrounds Catania only adds to its allure. Mount Etna, the most active volcano in Europe, is a commanding but alluring sight that dominates the skyline. This magnificent natural beauty may be seen from Catania's streets and squares, serving as a daily reminder of the city's special geographic location. Urban life and the unbridled power of nature interact to produce an atmosphere that is both awe-inspiring and alluring.

Catania has a long and rich history, with remnants of many different civilizations visible all over the place. Its streets' baroque construction is a tribute to the city's fortitude in the face of calamities like earthquakes and volcanic eruptions. Catania's focal point, Piazza del Duomo, is home to the Cathedral of Sant'Agata, which honors the city's patron saint, as well as the recognizable Fontana dell'Elefante, a symbol of Catania.

Catania thrives as a contemporary cultural center while still embracing its past. With theaters, galleries, and cultural institutions that hold a range of concerts, exhibitions, and events, the city is home to a thriving arts scene. These cultural attractions give tourists the chance to interact with modern manifestations of Sicilian creativity and tradition.

Food lovers will enjoy Catania's gastronomic scene. The city's proximity to the ocean guarantees a consistent supply of fresh seafood, which appears on local menus in a variety of mouthwatering dishes. Catania's culinary environment, which offers a delectable tour of Sicilian food, reflects the region's distinctive flavors and traditions in everything from pasta to pastries.

In conclusion, Catania is a city that successfully fuses its ancient past with a modern, energetic current. A lovely location that perfectly represents Sicilian life is created by vibrant marketplaces, breathtaking Mount Etna views, and a rich cultural tapestry. Catania offers a genuine and remarkable experience for anyone looking to immerse themselves in the heart of

Sicily, whether they choose to explore its markets, adore its architecture, or indulge in its food.

agrigento: valley of the temples

Agrigento, a charming city on Sicily's southern coast, is well-known for its unique historical location known as the "Valley of the Temples." Visitors may take an amazing trip back in time at this UNESCO World Heritage Site, which is a testimony to ancient Greek culture and architecture.

The Valley of the Temples, also known as "Valle dei Templi" in Italian, is a large archaeological site that contains several extremely well-preserved ancient Greek temples. When

Agrigento, formerly known as Akragas, was a thriving Greek colony, these temples were constructed in the 5th century BC. Visitors from all over the world are continually enthralled by the site's captivating fusion of myth, history, and creativity.

The Temple of Concordia, a flawlessly maintained Doric temple that serves as one of the best specimens of Greek architecture, is the valley of the temples' main attraction. The craftsmanship of the time is evident in its elegant columns and delicate detailing. Other notable buildings that accentuate the environment with their commanding presence are the Temple of Heracles and the Temple of Juno, both of which are devoted to the goddess Hera.

The Valley of the Temples transports tourists to a time of opulence and devotion as they stroll through it. Awe and astonishment are sparked by the monuments' immense size when viewed against the backdrop of the Sicilian landscape. The ancient Greeks would have assembled for ceremonies and rituals in honor of their gods, one can imagine when strolling along the walkways.

The Valley of the Temples offers expansive vistas of the surrounding countryside and the glistening Mediterranean Sea beyond the actual temples. The harmonious coexistence of architectural wonders and scenic splendor fosters a meditative mood that invites visitors to think back on the passage of time and the lasting impact of ancient civilizations.

A trip to the Valley of the Temples is an educational tour through history and culture. The museum at the location enhances the overall experience by adding more context and knowledge about the history, relics, and setting of the temples. The beautiful ceramics, sculptures, and other objects on display provide visitors an insight into the customs and way of life of the people who once called this ancient metropolis home.

Finally, the Valley of the Temples in Agrigento serves as a testament to Greek civilization and artistic skill. With its magnificent temples and atmospheric environs, Sicily offers a singular chance to connect with the past and learn more about its lengthy history. The Valley of the Temples offers a unique experience for anybody interested in history, architecture, or simply in immersing themselves in the grandeur of the past.

Syracuse: Ancient Greek and Roman Treasures

Syracuse, which is tucked away on Sicily's southeast coast, stands as a living example of the magnificence of the classical Greek and Roman worlds. Syracuse is a treasure mine of archaeological wonders that capture the imagination, with a history spanning centuries and a heritage that has left an unmistakable effect on the area.

The Archaeological Park of Neapolis is located in the center of Syracuse's historical wealth. This expansive location encourages tourists to travel back in time and discover the ruins of a long-ago era. Once upon a time, the Greek Theater, a famous building carved from the stone of the nearby hills, echoed with the voices of actors and audiences, fostering an environment of creative and social connection. Incorporating mystery and intrigue, The Ear of Dionysius, a limestone cave renowned for its exceptional acoustics, transports visitors to a world of ethereal whispers.

Within the same park, the Roman Amphitheater provides a taste of the splendor of Roman entertainment and engineering prowess. Its seating tiers and architectural style bring to mind the events and competitions that formerly attracted city people. The Altar of Hieron II, which is close by, serves as a reminder of the centrality of ritual in ancient Syracuse and a witness to the city's historical and religious customs.

A fascinating blend of architectural styles and cultural influences may be seen on the island of Ortygia, which is where Syracuse's ancient center is located. The Cathedral of Syracuse is located in Piazza del Duomo and is surrounded by Baroque and medieval structures. The cathedral's evolution over time, from its beginnings as a Greek temple honoring Athena, represents the layers of history that make up the city. The Fountain of Arethusa, a peaceful haven nearby with a freshwater spring rumored to be connected to the Greek nymph Arethusa, is a place of myth and truth.

The archaeological gems of Syracuse extend beyond its parks and historic areas. The Paolo Orsi Archaeological Museum is home to an outstanding collection of artifacts that illustrate the various facets of Syracuse's prehistoric culture. The museum provides a thorough picture of the city's rich past, including everything from beautiful sculptures and pottery to inscriptions and commonplace items.

In conclusion, Syracuse serves as a live example of the lasting contributions made by the ancient Greek and Roman cultures. Together, the Paolo Orsi Archaeological Museum, the island of Ortygia, and the Archaeological Park of Neapolis offer a comprehensive look into Syracuse's cultural heritage. Syracuse offers a fascinating experience that connects the current world and the echoes of antiquity, whether it be meandering through historic theaters, astonishment at architectural changes, or immersion in historical objects.

CHAPTER 3 Natural Wonders

Mount Etna: Europe's Tallest Active Volcano

The tallest active volcano in Europe is Mount Etna, a towering presence on the Sicilian island. This well-known natural phenomenon serves as a metaphor for both nature's untamed force and breathtaking beauty.

Mount Etna dominates the Sicilian skyline and acts as a constant reminder of the island's volcanic history, magnificently rising to an elevation of nearly 3,300 meters (10,900 ft). Its history of eruptions dates back thousands of years, and its fiery outbursts have left their mark on Sicily's terrain and populace.

The appeal of Mount Etna goes beyond its commanding size. From lush woods to bizarre lava fields, the environment is home to a wide variety of habitats. Sicily's reputation as a place of exceptional cuisine is largely due to the volcanic soils, which have fostered the establishment of wineries, orchards, and farms. Charming towns and villages in the surrounding area can be found that have adapted to the difficulties and opportunities presented by residing so near to an active volcano.

Mount Etna is a wonderful laboratory for the study of geology and volcanism for academics and researchers. Insights into the interior workings of the Earth and how geological forces form the planet's surface are gained from its regular eruptions. Even while the volcano's activity has the potential to be harmful, it also draws specialists from all over the world who want to learn more about and forecast volcanic behavior.

Because of its distinctive blend of natural beauty and adrenaline, Mount Etna attracts tourists and adventure seekers. The lower slopes may be explored, the effects of previous eruptions can be seen, and the volcanic sceneries can be marveled at on guided tours and treks. To experience the steam vents, craters, and spectacular panoramic vistas up close, adventurous visitors can even climb to the summit region.

The eruptions of Mount Etna serve as a constant reminder of the Earth's dynamic nature and ongoing change. Local towns may have difficulties as a result of the volcano's activity, but it also adds to the rich fabric of Sicilian culture and identity. Its potent and alluring presence continues to leave a lasting impression on those who are fortunate enough to witness it.

In conclusion, Mount Etna, the tallest active volcano in Europe, àis distinguished out for its commanding presence and dynamic character. It functions as an enthralling natural landmark, a subject of scholarly investigation, and a representation of the complex interrelationship between geological processes and human existence.

Aeolian Islands: Unspoiled Paradise

Despite the fact that each of the Aeolian Islands is unique, they all have a certain untouched appeal in common. Every feature of these islands appears to have been undisturbed by time and technology, from the spectacular vistas to the pristine waters.

The active volcano on Stromboli also referred to as the "Lighthouse of the Mediterranean," is renowned for its intermittent bursts of lava fire and continual soft stream of smoke. Black sand beaches and the mountainous topography of this island give the surroundings an unearthly feel.

The Aeolian Island of Panarea, the smallest and presumably most exclusive, emanates a sense of refinement and leisure. White-washed homes, picturesque villages, and opulent resorts all contribute to the area's affluent calm.

For travelers looking for a more leisurely pace, Salina's rich vegetation and beautiful towns provide a picturesque background. A local treat that enhances the sensory delights of a trip to Salina is the sweet Malvasia wine, which is produced in the island's vineyards.

The most populous of the Aeolian Islands, Lipari, is a center of activity and culture. In stark contrast to the tranquil serenity of the surrounding sea and countryside are its busy streets, historical landmarks, and colorful markets.

Due to its beautiful craters, hot springs, and mud baths, Vulcano, which was appropriately called after the Roman god of fire, exhibits its volcanic origin. Unique wellness experiences are provided by its geothermal attractions.

Among the Aeolian Islands, Filicudi and Alicudi are the more isolated islands that draw travelers looking for a true getaway from contemporary life. These islands provide a chance to unplug and experience unspoiled nature.

Divers and snorkelers will find the Aeolian Islands to be a paradise because of their immaculate beauty underwater as well. A fascinating underwater world that is just waiting to be discovered is made up of vibrant marine life, underground tunnels, and pure waters.

The unspoiled paradise experience is completed with the islands' genuine culture and cuisine. Local eateries offer traditional Sicilian fare with a distinctive Aeolian flavor. The islanders' kindness and warmth offer a unique personal touch that improves the island experience.

The Aeolian Islands, in sum, genuinely live up to their image as an "unspoiled paradise." These islands offer an escape that seems to take place in another era because of their spectacular landscapes, clean oceans, peaceful settlements, and rich cultures. The Aeolian Islands offer a memorable retreat from the every day, whether travelers are looking for adventure, relaxation, or a look at real island life.

Zingaro Nature Reserve: Coastal Hiking and Scenery

A refuge of peace and stunning scenery may be found in the Zingaro Nature Reserve, which is situated along Sicily's northwest coast. Visitors can enjoy breathtaking coastal trekking and spectacular views in this protected region, which spans over 7 kilometers (4.3 miles) of rough shoreline.

A world of pristine landscapes and thriving biodiversity welcomes you as soon as you enter the Zingaro Nature Reserve. The reserve serves as a haven for a broad variety of plants and animals, including rare plant species and a wide range of marine life. A visually captivating symphony is produced by the combination of craggy cliffs, blue waters, and lush flora.

The network of hiking trails that wind through the diverse topography of the Zingaro Nature Reserve is one of its great attractions. The reserve is accessible to both casual walkers and seasoned hikers thanks to the varied difficulty levels of the pathways. Each path offers a different view of the reserve's magnificence, whether it is expansive panoramas from high vantage points or the chance to discover secret coves and secluded beaches.

The coastline's trails show an enthralling interaction between land and sea. The Mediterranean's emerald waters contrast with the region's towering cliffs, providing a beautiful setting for your adventure. Your journey will be even more exciting if you happen to spot any aquatic creatures along the way, such as dolphins or sea turtles.

For those who love the outdoors and take pictures, the Zingaro Nature Reserve is a veritable paradise. There are countless opportunities to take breathtaking photos thanks to the variety of settings, which range from rocky cliffs to serene beaches. The pathways' various turns and turns reveal fresh perspectives that arouse surprise and a love of the natural world.

The Zingaro Nature Reserve offers an amazing experience, regardless of your preference for solitude, adventure, or a close relationship with nature. Your interaction with the reserve will be authentic and undisturbed because there aren't any enormous crowds or commercial development there. You are invited to immerse yourself in the sights, sounds, and scents of nature in this beautiful setting, which provides a welcome break from the stress of daily life.

Let's sum up by saying that the Zingaro Nature Reserve is a seaside treasure that entices visitors to explore its untamed pathways and breathtaking landscape. For those seeking the beauty and tranquility of untainted nature, the reserve offers a revitalizing vacation with its varied landscapes, abundant biodiversity, and sense of serene seclusion.

CHAPTER 4 Immersive Cultural Experiences

Local Festivals and Celebrations

Sicily is known for its vibrant and diverse festivals that celebrate its rich cultural heritage, history, and traditions. These festivals offer a unique opportunity to immerse yourself in local customs, taste traditional foods, and experience the lively atmosphere that characterizes Sicilian life. Here are some notable local festivals and celebrations in Sicily:

1. Sagra del Mandorlo in Fiore (Almond Blossom Festival): Held in Agrigento in late February or early March, this festival celebrates the blooming almond trees with parades, concerts, and cultural events. The picturesque landscape

becomes a sea of white and pink blossoms.

2. Sagra del Pesce (Fish Festival): A celebrated event in Aci Trezza, near Catania, this festival usually takes place in June. It features a seafood feast, boat parades, music, and dance, all honoring the town's strong maritime heritage.

3. Festa di Santa Rosalia (Feast of Saint Rosalia): The patron saint of Palermo, Saint Rosalia, is celebrated in July with a grand procession through the city. The event involves religious ceremonies, fireworks, and street parties.

4. Festa di Sant'Agata (Feast of Saint Agatha): Also in Catania, this religious festival in February honors Saint Agatha, the city's patron saint. The festivities include processions, candlelit vigils, and the traditional "cannolo a forma di

mammella" (cannoli shaped like a breast) pastry.

Infiorata di Noto (Noto Flower Festival):In May, the streets of Noto are transformed into intricate and colorful flower carpets. The event showcases elaborate designs created entirely from petals, celebrating spring and the artistry of the locals.

1. Festa della Madonna della Luce (Festival of Our Lady of Light): Celebrated in August in Caltagirone, this festival features a stunning procession of candles and torches, illuminating the city's famous ceramic-decorated staircases.

2. Settimana Santa (Holy Week): Easter celebrations in Sicily are marked by elaborate processions, particularly in Enna, Trapani, and

Caltanissetta. These processions depict the Passion of Christ and are deeply rooted in religious tradition.

3. Festa di San Giuseppe (Feast of Saint Joseph): Celebrated across the island on March 19th, this festival involves creating elaborate altars adorned with flowers, bread, and pastries as an offering to Saint Joseph.

4. Cous Cous Fest: This international food festival takes place in San Vito Lo Capo in September. It celebrates cultural diversity through couscous dishes from various countries, along with music, workshops, and exhibitions.

5. Sagra del Grano (Wheat Festival): In August, the town of Cerda hosts a festival to honor its

agricultural roots, showcasing traditional Sicilian wheat-based products and culture.

These are just a few examples of the many festivals that take place throughout the year in Sicily. Keep in mind that festival dates and details might change, so it's advisable to check local sources or tourism websites for the most up-to-date information before planning your visit.

Traditional Cuisine and Local Delicacies

Sicilian cuisine is a delightful fusion of flavors influenced by its history, geography, and cultural heritage. The island's traditional dishes incorporate fresh ingredients, aromatic herbs, and a mix of Mediterranean and Arabic influences. Here are some iconic Sicilian dishes and local delicacies you should try when visiting:

1. Arancini: These fried rice balls are a popular snack or street food. They're typically stuffed with various fillings like ragù (meat sauce), mozzarella, and peas, then coated with breadcrumbs and fried to perfection.
2. Caponata: A flavorful eggplant-based dish cooked with tomatoes, olives, capers, onions, and celery. It's often served as an appetizer or side dish.
3. Pasta alla Norma: A pasta dish featuring tomato sauce, eggplant, basil, and ricotta salata (a type of dried, salted ricotta cheese).
4. Sicilian Pizza (Sfincione): A thick, spongy pizza topped with tomato sauce, onions,

breadcrumbs, and sometimes cheese. It's a beloved street food in Sicily.

5. Sarde a Beccafico: Stuffed sardines filled with a mixture of breadcrumbs, pine nuts, raisins, parsley, and garlic, then baked or fried.

6. Pasta con le Sarde: A pasta dish made with bucatini (a thick, hollow spaghetti), sardines, wild fennel, saffron, and pine nuts.

7. Cassata: A sweet dessert made with ricotta cheese, sugar, candied fruit, and sponge cake, all encased in marzipan. It's often decorated with colorful icing and intricate designs.

8. Cannoli: Crispy pastry tubes filled with sweet ricotta cheese and often adorned with candied fruit or chocolate chips.

9. Granita: A refreshing, semi-frozen dessert made from sugar, water, and

flavorings like lemon, coffee, or almond. It's commonly enjoyed with a brioche bun for breakfast.

10. Pistachios: Sicily is known for its high-quality pistachios, used in various dishes and desserts, including pistachio gelato and pastries.
11. Cuddiruni: A deep-fried dough pocket filled with chickpeas, onion, and other seasonings. It's a popular street food, especially during festivals.
12. Pani ca Meusa: A sandwich filled with sautéed veal spleen and lung, often served with cheese and lemon.
13. Panelle: Fried chickpea fritters that are crispy on the outside and soft on the inside, often served in a roll as a sandwich.
14. Buccellato: A sweet ring-shaped bread filled with dried figs, raisins, nuts, and

other ingredients. It's a specialty during Christmas and other festive occasions.

Sicilian cuisine is an exploration of flavors, with an emphasis on fresh and seasonal ingredients. Be sure to explore local markets, trattorias, and street food stalls to fully savor the unique tastes of Sicily. Remember that each region of the island has its own specialties and variations, so don't hesitate to try dishes specific to the area you're visiting.

Sicilian Wines and Vineyards

Sicily is a renowned region for its wine production, boasting a diverse range of grape varieties and wine styles. The island's climate, rich soil, and proximity to the Mediterranean Sea create ideal conditions for grape cultivation. Here are some notable Sicilian wines and regions you should explore:

1. Nero d'Avola: This red wine grape is considered the most important indigenous variety of Sicily. Wines made from Nero d'Avola grapes are known for their rich, full-bodied character, often with dark fruit flavors and hints of spices.
2. Etna Rosso: Produced on the slopes of Mount Etna, Europe's tallest active volcano, this red wine showcases the volcanic terroir. It's often a blend of Nerello Mascalese and Nerello Cappuccio grapes, resulting in elegant, mineral-driven wines.
3. Marsala: This fortified wine hails from the town of Marsala on the western coast of Sicily. It comes in various styles, from

dry to sweet, and is often used in cooking as well as enjoyed as an aperitif.

4. Grillo: A white grape variety that produces crisp, aromatic white wines with citrus and floral notes. It's used both in still wines and in blends for Marsala production.

5. Cerasuolo di Vittoria: A red wine from the region of Ragusa, this is Sicily's only DOCG (Denominazione di Origine Controllata e Garantita) wine. It's a blend of Nero d'Avola and Frappato grapes, resulting in a balanced and elegant wine.

6. Passito di Pantelleria: Pantelleria, a small island off the coast of Sicily, produces this sweet wine made from sun-dried Zibibbo (Muscat of Alexandria) grapes. It's a luscious dessert wine with notes of dried fruits and honey.

7. Catarratto: The most widely planted white grape variety in Sicily, Catarratto is used to produce a range of white wines from light and fresh to more structured and complex.
8. Malvasia delle Lipari: Another sweet wine specialty, this is produced on the Aeolian Islands. It's made from Malvasia grapes and offers a harmonious blend of sweetness and acidity. When visiting Sicily, you have the opportunity to explore many vineyards and wineries across the island. The region around Mount Etna, for example, has become a hotspot for wine tourism, offering picturesque landscapes and unique wine experiences. Many wineries offer tastings, tours, and the chance to learn about the winemaking process.

Whether you're a wine enthusiast or simply interested in trying local flavors, Sicilian wines provide a taste of the island's terroir and history, making your culinary journey in Sicily even more memorable

CHAPTER 5 Historical Sites and Architecture

Norman Cathedrals and Arab-Norman Palaces

The Arab-Norman history of Sicily is a magnificent assemblage of architectural gems. This UNESCO World Heritage site displays how the historical architecture of the island combines Arab, Byzantine, and Norman influences. Beautiful cathedrals and palaces are among the magnificent Arab-Norman structures that showcase Sicily's medieval cultural diversity and aesthetic triumphs.

The Cathedral of Cefalù, one of the Norman cathedrals, was constructed in the 12th century and combines Byzantine and Norman elements. Beautiful mosaics that depict biblical scenes are used to decorate the inside.

Monreale Cathedral is a marvel of Norman architecture and is well-known for its stunning golden mosaics. The mosaics tell biblical tales and reveal information about the area's cultural past.

Cathedral of Palermo (Cattedrale di Palermo): This cathedral is a stunning example of a fusion of architectural styles, drawing inspiration from the Norman, Gothic, and Baroque periods. Its varied features are a reflection of the island's historical development.

Arab-Norman Palaces: Palazzo dei Normanni, also called the Royal Palace of Palermo, was built by the Arabs at first and afterward enlarged by the Normans. It is home to the magnificent Palatine Chapel, famous for its elaborate mosaics.

Zisa Palace: This Arab-Norman palace in Palermo is a striking example of how Islamic and Norman architectural styles can coexist. Beautiful gardens and elaborate ornamentation can be found there.

Cuba Palace: This modest palace, which can be found in Palermo, exhibits Arab elements in its architecture. It is thought that the Arabic term "Qubba," which means dome, is where the name "Cuba" originates.

Palermo's Chiaramonte Palace (Palazzo Chiaramonte-Steri) is a palace that illustrates the change from the Norman to the Gothic era. It is renowned for originally blending several architectural styles.

These buildings provide evidence of Sicily's peaceful intercultural interaction and coexistence during the Middle Ages. The island's history is well represented by the Arab-Norman heritage, which also serves as a showcase for the creative and architectural innovations brought about by this fusion of cultures. Discovering the beauty and complexity of this distinctive architectural legacy can be done by touring Sicily's cathedrals and palaces.

Segesta: Ancient Temple and Theater

Its ancient temple and theater are extraordinarily well-preserved, and Segesta, an old city in western Sicily, is well-known for them. These archeological sites provide a window into the area's illustrious past and distinctive architecture.

Segesta Temple: The Segesta Temple is one of the best-preserved ancient Greek temples still standing. It is perched on a hilltop with a view of the countryside. The temple, which is devoted to a god who is unknown, is thought to have been built by the Elymian people. It has fourteen columns on the long sides and six columns on the short sides, all of which are Doric in style. The temple is a monument to old craftsmanship and architectural design even if it was never finished. The temple's isolated and gorgeous setting contributes to the sense of awe it inspires.

The Segesta Theater, which is located next to the temple, is another noteworthy feature of the archeological site. This Greek-style theater is in excellent condition and was built into the hill's natural slope. The theater offers not only historical information but also a wonderful performance space with its gorgeous backdrop of the surrounding countryside. In antiquity, the theater was utilized for a variety of cultural events and theatrical performances, and it could hold up to 4,000 spectators.

Travelers can take a trip back in time and admire the architectural prowess of past civilizations by going to Segesta. The tranquil environment and expansive vistas of the Sicilian countryside improve the overall experience. A deeper understanding of the region's cultural and historical context can be gained from exploring the temple and theater, as well as a respect for the timeless beauty of historic buildings. A trip to Segesta is gratifying and educational, regardless of whether you're a history buff, an architecture aficionado, or just interested in Sicily's past.

Selinunte: Greek Ruins by the Sea

In southwest Sicily, Selinunte is a remarkable archaeological site that displays the remnants of a prehistoric Greek city encircled by breathtaking coastal vistas. Selinunte's ruins give an enthralling view of the magnificence and historical significance of this formerly bustling city.

Selinunte in the past:

Greek colonists from Megara Hyblaea founded Selinunte in the seventh century BC, and it grew to be one of the most significant Greek colonies in Sicily. Due to its abundant olive groves and fertile grounds, the city prospered as a hub of trade and agriculture. It also had a significant role in the local wars that were common in the ancient Mediterranean region.

Temples and Ruins:

The Selinunte archeological site is home to a number of magnificent Doric temples and ruins that shed light on the city's architectural and cultural history. Among notable constructions are:

Temple E: Also referred to as the Temple of Hera, this enormous structure is one of the biggest Greek temples ever built. Its towering columns and other remnants give visitors a feel of the city's grand architecture.

Temple C: This shrine to Athena offers breathtaking panoramas of the ocean and surroundings. Visitors can now get a glimpse of the temple's former splendor thanks to partial restoration.

Acropolis: The region surrounding the towering acropolis displays the remains of numerous temples, shrines, and public structures. It provides vistas of the surrounding countryside and the sea in all directions.

Agora: The central market of the city, the agora, once served as a center of activity and trade.

The ruins of its structures and columns provide a window into daily life in prehistoric Selinunte.

The Mediterranean Sea's proximity to Selinunte is one of the city's most alluring features. Ancient ruins set against the background of glistening blue waters produce a wonderfully magnificent and evocative ambiance. A unique experience that combines history and environment is provided by the opportunity to explore the ancient site before relaxing on the surrounding beach.

Travelers can experience a sense of time travel, envision the vibrant life of an ancient Greek city, and take in the timeless beauty of the Sicilian coast by visiting Selinunte. The location is a must-visit location for anybody interested in history, archaeology, or the stunning Sicilian landscapes due to its historical significance, architectural marvels, and natural environs.

CHAPTER 6 Outdoor Activities

Beaches and Water SportsHiking and Trekking Routes

Beaches and Water Sports:

Beaches and Water Activities: Sicily is recognized for its breathtaking coastline and immaculate beaches that can accommodate a variety of tastes, from leisurely sunbathing to active water activities. Sicily has a number of well-liked beaches and opportunities for water sports, including:

The picturesque San Vito Lo Capo Beach is known for its pristine white sand and crystal-clear blue seas. It's a well-liked location for sunbathing, swimming, and snorkeling.

Isola Bella Beach is a small island that is close to Taormina and is connected to the mainland by a slender stretch of land. Swimming and water sports like kayaking and paddleboarding are both highly recommended at the beach.

Mondello Beach in Palermo is a broad, sandy beach with calm waters that is ideal for kids. Beach volleyball and windsurfing are also very popular there.

On the island of Favignana, Cala Rossa is renowned for its pristine waters and underwater caverns. Here, diving and snorkeling are common pastimes.

Cefalù Beach: This beach, which is tucked behind the town's old cathedral, provides a gorgeous environment for swimming and tanning.

Water Sports: Along the Sicilian coast, you can engage in scuba diving, snorkeling, windsurfing, kiteboarding, and sailing.

Hiking and Trekking Routes:

Sicily's varied terrain provides a wealth of hiking and trekking options, allowing outdoor enthusiasts to explore its mountains, hills, and countryside. Routes for notable hikes and treks include:

The tallest active volcano in Europe, Mount Etna, provides a variety of hiking routes, from simpler trails to more difficult ascents. Black lava fields and expansive views make the surroundings seem fantastical.

The Zingaro Nature Reserve is a coastal nature reserve with well-marked hiking trails that wind along craggy cliffs, immaculate beaches, and turquoise waters.

Nebrodi Mountains: The Nebrodi Regional Park has a number of hiking paths that wind through valleys, woodlands, and agricultural settings.

The Madonie Mountains: The Madonie Regional Natural Park has a wide variety of plants and animals and provides routes that lead to scenic towns, waterfalls, and vista points.

Natural pools, gorgeous coastal pathways, and opportunities to witness local species can all be found in the Riserva Naturale Orientata dello Zingaro.

The limestone cliffs of Scala dei Turchi near Agrigento offer a distinctive scenery to explore and appreciate, despite the fact that they are not a common hiking route.

Sicily provides a variety of possibilities for outdoor enthusiasts and environment lovers, whether you're looking for leisure on gorgeous beaches, water sports experiences, or the thrill of discovering magnificent hiking paths. Just keep in mind to check the most recent details and weather forecasts for the activities and routes you're interested in before starting your excursion.

Cycling Tours and Routes

Cycling aficionados will love Sicily's varied topography, quaint villages, and stunning seaside views. Cycling excursions and routes are available for all skill levels and interests, whether you're a casual or competitive rider. Here are some suggested cycling routes and tours in Sicily:

Eastern Sicily Coastal Route: From Catania, ride through Sicily's beautiful eastern coast, passing through quaint communities like Taormina and Siracusa. Along the trip, take in the breathtaking coastal views, historical landmarks, and regional food.

Take a ferry to the Aeolian Islands, a volcanic archipelago off the northern coast of Sicily, for an excursion. Cycle across the islands, stopping at Lipari, Salina, and Vulcano, and take in the distinctive scenery and native culture.

The Western Sicily Loop passes through Trapani, Marsala, and Selinunte as it travels through the western portion of the island.

Historic attractions, vineyards, and coastal towns are all accessible for exploration.

Ride across the countryside in Val di Noto, an area renowned for its Baroque cities and undulating vistas. Starting in Noto, cycle through quaint towns like Modica and Ragusa.

Cycling Mount Etna: The ascent of Mount Etna offers more experienced cyclists a difficult route with excellent panoramic vistas. Select a route based on your level of fitness and expertise from the route's various degrees of difficulty.

Ride past Sicilian Wine Country: Combine wine tasting with cycling on a tour that passes past vineyards and wineries in regions like the countryside of Trapani. While sipping local wines, take in the panoramic splendor of the surroundings.

Follow the Sicilian Baroque Towns Trail to bicycle through the UNESCO-listed Baroque towns of southeast Sicily. Experience the architectural magnificence and culinary delights of Modica, Ragusa, and Scicli as you travel through these cities.

North Coast Adventure: Travel along the northern coast beginning in Palermo, and going past coastal towns, olive gardens, and citrus farms. The scenery along this route alternates between rural and coastal vistas.

Make sure you are prepared, have the necessary safety gear, and have a reliable map or navigation app before beginning any bicycle tour or route. Additionally, be careful of the road conditions and local traffic laws. Some routes could be better suited for mountain bikes because of their difficult terrain. Making the most of your riding trip in Sicily requires preparation, route selection, and consideration of your fitness level and interests.

CHAPTER 7 Practical Tips for Travelers

Language and Communication

As in the rest of Italy, Italian is the major language used in Sicily. But it's important to know that some people also speak Sicilian as a second language or in casual settings. Sicilian is a distinctive Romance language with influences from numerous historical eras and civilizations. Sicilian is frequently used in casual chats with family and friends, although Italian is the language of official correspondence, academic instruction, business, and tourism.

When visiting Sicily, being able to communicate in daily situations and respect the local way of life can be made much easier by learning a few fundamental Italian words. Some useful expressions include the following:

Hello: Informally, say "hello" or "buongiorno."

Goodbye: Arrivederci

Please: Thanks a lot

Many thanks. Grazie

Greetings to you: Prego

Yes: Sì

No: No

I'm sorry. Sorry: Mi scusi (formal) or Scusa (informal)

Parli inglese: Do you speak English?

I fail to grasp: not a capisce

The cost is: Quanto costa?

Where are you: Dove si trova?

Bathrooms: Bagno

Even though many persons working in the tourism sector, particularly in well-known locations, speak English to varied degrees, it is polite and appreciated to attempt to speak Italian whenever you can. During your stay in Sicily, using fundamental words and expressions can greatly improve relationships and help you have moments you'll never forget. For more difficult interactions, having a phrasebook or a translation tool handy can be a helpful backup.

Safety and Health Considerations

As with any destination, it's crucial to put safety and health first when visiting Sicily if you want your trip to go smoothly and be pleasurable. Here are some things to keep in mind about health and safety:

Basic Security: Be careful: Especially in congested places and popular tourist destinations, pay attention to your surroundings. To avoid theft, keep a close eye on your possessions.

Know your neighborhood's emergency phone numbers, including those for the police (113), medical (118), and fire departments (115).

Local ordinances and practices: Consider the local customs and laws. When touring religious landmarks, dress modestly.

Transportation Safety: If taking a rental car or other form of public transportation, abide by the regulations of the road and drive carefully.

Swimming in uncharted seas should be done with caution. Pay heed to caution signs and obey the lifeguard's directions.

Considering health:

Make sure you have complete travel insurance that covers medical emergencies, trip cancellations, and other unanticipated circumstances.

Medical Care: Become familiar with where the local hospitals and clinics are located before you travel. The majority of major cities have hospitals and clinics.

Prescription drugs: If you need to take prescription drugs, make sure you pack enough of them and keep your prescription with you. It's possible that some drugs go by various names in Italy.

Food & Water Safety: While most locations of Sicily's tap water are typically safe to drink, tourists may prefer bottled water because it is freely available. Choose reputable restaurants instead of eating on the street.

Sun protection is essential given Sicily's bright weather. To prevent heat-related problems, use sunscreen, put on a hat, sunglasses, and water.

Protect yourself against insects: Insects may be present depending on the time of year and where you are. To avoid bites, apply insect repellent.

Wellness precautions: According to the laws of your own country, find out if any vaccines are required before visiting Sicily.

COVID-19 Considerations (as of September 2021, when I last updated):

Check Entry Prerequisites: Be aware of any possible entry restrictions, such as testing or quarantine, relating to COVID-19.

Observe the rules: Follow local health regulations, which may include using masks and keeping a social distance when necessary.

Know Your Stuff: Keep abreast of any COVID-19 developments as well as any travel warnings issued by your government or medical institutions.

Keep in mind that health and safety regulations can change, so it's crucial to stay updated and adjust your preparations as necessary. It will be easier to guarantee a secure and happy time in Sicily if you check with trustworthy sources both before and during your trip.

Locals Etiquette and Customs

It will make your trip to Sicily more pleasurable and culturally sensitive if you are aware of and respect local customs and etiquette. Here are a few things to think about:

The customary way to greet someone when you first meet them is with a handshake.

Prior to being asked to use their first name, use their titles (e.g., "Signora" for a woman and

"Signore" for a man) followed by their last names.

While on-time arrival is welcomed, social events and business meetings in Italy can have a more relaxed pace.

Dress modestly when visiting places of worship by covering your shoulders and avoiding short skirts or shorts.

Italians are etiquette-conscious when it comes to dining. Before you start, wait until the host has finished eating.

It's customary to consume every bite of food on your plate because leaving any behind can be viewed as wasteful.

Italians enjoy their coffee very much, but you should know that they usually drink cappuccinos in the morning. Later in the day, pick espresso or another type of coffee.

Tipping: Although a service fee (coperto) is frequently added to the tab at restaurants, giving a small gratuity is still appreciated. Leave a few euros or round up.

Even while tipping is less popular than in some other nations, it is nevertheless a lovely gesture for good service.

Speaking loudly in public, especially inside, is considered unfriendly behavior.

If you don't know your conversation partner well, stay away from sensitive subjects like politics or religion.

Greetings and Goodbyes: In casual circumstances, "Ciao" is frequently used for both hello and goodbye.

Close friends and family will frequently greet each other by kissing them on the cheeks, beginning on the left.

Although Italian is widely spoken, some inhabitants may also speak Sicilian. Respect for the community can be demonstrated by using simple Italian phrases.

Bringing a small present, such as a box of chocolates, a bottle of wine, or some flowers, is welcomed when you are invited to someone's home. Italians are known for their passionate chats and debates. With excitement and an open mind, participate.

Relaxation and Family Time: Sundays are frequently used for relaxing with family members. There may be a lot of closed or irregularly open stores and companies.

Recognizing and adjusting to local customs is a good idea because, as we all know, cultural norms might differ. In general, respecting regional traditions and customs will help you engage with Sicilian culture and foster pleasant interactions there.

CHAPTER 8 Recommended Itineraries

5-Day Cultural Exploration

Sicily's rich history, architecture, gastronomy, and landscapes can all be experienced during a 5-day cultural journey of the island. To maximize your cultural tour, follow this suggested itinerary:

Palermo, a historical splendor, Day 1

Arrive at Sicily's capital, Palermo.

Visit the Palazzo dei Normanni, where you can see the magnificent Palatine Chapel with its elaborate mosaics.

To discover regional cuisines and goods, explore the lively Ballar Market.

While eating a classic Sicilian meal, stroll around the old streets.

Day two: Cefalù and Monreale - Art and Coast

Visit Monreale to admire the spectacular cathedral's golden mosaics.

Observe the delicate architectural elements of the Cloister of Monreale.

Explore the quaint village of Cefalù with its stunning cathedral and beaches by taking a drive there.

Agrigento's Ancient Wonders on Day 3

Visit Agrigento and take a tour of the UNESCO World Heritage site known as the Valley of the Temples.

Observe the well-maintained Greek temples and ruins.

Enjoy a calm evening in Agrigento, a city renowned for its old-world charm.

Syracuse - Ancient and Medieval on Day 4

Take a trip to Syracuse's Archaeological Park, which features a stunning Greek Theater and Roman Amphitheater.

Discover the enchanting Ortigia island, renowned for its vibrant atmosphere and antique buildings.

Visit the Syracuse Cathedral and the Arethusa Fountain.

Taormina and Mount Etna on Day 5: Culture and Nature

To see Taormina, a charming town renowned for its historic theater and breathtaking scenery, take a drive there.

If time permits, go on a trip to Mount Etna, Europe's tallest active volcano, for a distinctive experience. Explore the Greek-Roman Theater and meander through the picturesque alleyways.

The combination of historical landmarks, architectural marvels, seaside splendor, and natural landscapes on this itinerary will give you a thorough understanding of Sicilian culture. Do not forget to change the itinerary to reflect your preferences and the precise opening times of the attractions. Consider scheduling guided excursions as well for greater insights into the regional history and culture.

7-Day Adventure and Nature Tour

Sicily's many landscapes may be explored, outdoor activities can be enjoyed, and the island's natural beauty can be appreciated on a 7-day adventure and nature tour. A proposed schedule for a thrilling and active week is provided below:

Arrival in Palermo on Day 1

When you get there, check into your lodging in Palermo.

Discover the bustling marketplaces and historical sights of the city.

To begin your adventure, savor a typical Sicilian meal.

Zingaro Nature Reserve and Scenic Hike on Day 2

Visit the Zingaro Nature Reserve on the coast in the northwest.

Start a beautiful trek along a seaside path while admiring breathtaking sights and undiscovered coves.

Swim in the cool blue waters for some refreshing fun.

Stay the night close to the reserve.

Third day: diving in Ustica

Take a boat to Ustica Island, a haven for divers.

Spend the day underground, discovering undersea caverns and marine life while scuba diving in the pristine seas.

Enjoy the local seafood specialties while unwinding on the island.

Day Four: Investigate the Madonie Mountains.

To visit a beautiful natural location, take a drive to the Madonie Mountains.

Pick from a variety of paths through forests and meadows for hiking.

Try the local delicacies as you visit the quaint village of Castelbuono.

In the Madonie area, spend the night.

Day Five: Canyoning in Alcantara Gorge

Consider going canyoning at the Alcantara Gorge.

Swim in freshwater pools, traverse the tiny valleys, and rappel down waterfalls.

Enjoy the excitement of this distinctive outdoor adventure.

Day 6: Wine tasting and Mount Etna Trekking

The highest active volcano in Europe is Mount Etna; go there.

Explore craters and lava structures on a guided trekking excursion on the volcano's pathways.

To experience wine tasting, go to a nearby winery on the Etna hills.

In the evening, return to your lodging.

Coastal biking and departure on day seven

Spend the morning riding around the beautiful coastline paths close to your lodging.

Take in the stunning views of the sea and the countryside.

Take with you priceless memories of your Sicilian experience as you depart for the airport or your next location.

This program mixes exciting outdoor pursuits with chances to discover Sicily's natural splendors. Make careful to confirm the accessibility and operating times of attractions, as well as any required guided tours or equipment rentals, in advance. Always remember to observe safety precautions before engaging in any adventurous activity, and pack the necessary clothing and equipment.

10-Day Grand Tour of Sicily

Sicily's unique culture, history, landscapes, and food can all be experienced over a 10-day grand tour of the island. A suggested route for a thorough and immersive trip is provided below:

Arrival in Palermo on Day 1

Arrive at Sicily's capital, Palermo.

Take a look around the Palatine Chapel and the Palazzo dei Normanni.

Street cuisine may be enjoyed while strolling around the old streets.

Monreale and Cefalù on Day 2

To view the magnificent mosaics in the Monreale Cathedral, travel to Monreale.

Visit the picturesque town and beach of Cefalù by driving there.

Agrigento and the Valley of the Temples on Day 3

Visit Agrigento and take in the UNESCO-listed Valley of the Temples.

Observe the remains and temples of the Greeks.

Piazza Armerina and Ragusa on Day 4

Visit the mosaics in the well-preserved Roman Villa del Casale in Piazza Armerina.

Explore the Baroque buildings of Ragusa by continuing.

Day 5: Noto and Modica

Visit the renowned chocolate stores in Modica as you stroll through its lovely streets.

Visit the other Baroque city on the UNESCO list, Noto.

Syracuse and Ortigia Island on Day 6

Discover the Greek Theater and Roman Amphitheater in Syracuse's archaeological park.

Learn about Ortigia's ancient streets.

Seventh day: Mount Etna and Catania

Visit the bustling marketplaces and historic district of Catania.

Visit Mount Etna and engage in guided hiking.

Taormina and Giardini Naxos on Day 8

Discover Taormina's lovely town and its historic theater.

In the seaside community of Giardini Naxos, unwind.

Aeolian Islands excursion on Day 9

Travel to the Aeolian Islands for the day and stop in Lipari and Vulcano.

Take in the distinctive scenery and regional culture.

Day 10: Arrival back in Palermo then departure

re-enter Palermo.

On your final day, go back to your favorite locations or explore any new ones you missed.

Leave Sicily from Palermo with fond recollections of your amazing vacation.

This itinerary provides an in-depth look at Sicily's history, culture, architecture, and scenic splendor. Adapt the timetable based on your preferences and the hours that attractions are available. Booking guided tours for visits to historical places and outdoor excursions may give you a richer understanding of each destination. Be prepared to enjoy the variety of tastes and sensations that Sicily has to offer by packing correctly for the various weather conditions and activities.

CHAPTER 9 Useful Resources Accommodation Options

A variety of lodging choices are available in Sicily to accommodate various tastes and price ranges. You may choose from a wide range of accommodations on the island, from opulent hotels to quaint guesthouses. Some of the most well-liked lodging choices in Sicily are listed below:

Resorts and Inns:

Luxury Hotels: Sicily is home to a large number of five-star hotels with breathtaking vistas, first-rate facilities, and top-notch service. Choose from alternatives in Palermo, Taormina, and Syracuse, among other cities.

Beach Resorts: Beachfront hotels are located along the shore and provide access to the sea as well as opportunities for leisure and water sports.

Bed and Breakfasts (B&Bs): B&Bs offer a warm, customized environment. They frequently are housed in old structures and provide a flavor of regional friendliness.

Agriturismi (Farm Stays): Staying in agriturismi, or farm lodging, is a great way to experience rural life. Enjoy the peace and quiet of the countryside while dining on delicious, locally produced food.

Guesthouses and Inns: Guesthouses and inns provide a cozy, frequently inexpensive stay in a setting that is more personal than bigger hotels.

vacation Apartments and Villas: Families or groups can rent out a vacation apartment or villa. It gives you more room and the freedom to prepare your own meals.

Budget-friendly tourists may stay at a few hostels in Sicily. They're a terrific way to meet other travelers and cut back on hotel expenses.

Boutique Hotels: Boutique hotels provide a distinctive and fashionable experience. They frequently have unusual interior designs and offer individualized service.

Historical accommodations: Some lodgings are located in medieval monasteries or palaces, providing a window into the island's past.

Eco-Friendly Lodges: For tourists looking for environmentally friendly lodgings, there are eco-friendly lodges and establishments that prioritize minimizing their negative environmental effects.

Campgrounds and Glamping: If you love the outdoors, you might choose to stay in a campsite or a glamping site to be close to nature.

When selecting lodging, keep things like location, facilities, price, and the experience you desire in mind. To guarantee your preferred choice, making a reservation in advance is advised, particularly during busy travel times. To learn more about the caliber of the facilities and service, read reviews left by other visitors.

Tour Operators and Guides

By offering local knowledge, historical insights, and hassle-free travel arrangements, working with trustworthy tour operators and guides may improve your experience while experiencing Sicily. You may maximize your vacation by using the following tour companies and resources:

Viator: From outdoor adventures to city sightseeing tours, Viator provides a wide selection of tours and activities in Sicily. Through their website, you may read reviews, browse alternatives, and make direct reservations.

GetYourGuide: Like Viator, GetYourGuide offers a website where users can search for and reserve tours, excursions, and other activities throughout Sicily. It's an easy approach to look into different possibilities and discover things that interest you.

Context Travel: Context Travel provides in-depth, expert-led trips. Their small-group excursions emphasize art, history, and cultural encounters to give visitors a greater knowledge of the locations.

Etna Experience: Etna Experience provides guided hiking and jeep trips to Mount Etna for those who are interested in doing so. They provide a variety of activities and knowledgeable advisers for people of all ability levels.

From food and wine tours to cultural and historical excursions, Sicilian Secrets is a local tour company that provides a range of experiences in Sicily. They want to deliver genuine and immersive experiences.

Through its platform, Your Local Cousin, tourists may get in touch with local experts who can offer tailored suggestions and travel guidance. It's a terrific approach to acquire recommendations that aren't mainstream.

Private Guides: A private guide may personalize the trip to your interests if you're searching for a more individualized encounter. Online travel agencies like ToursByLocals and Withlocals match tourists with local tour operators.

Local Tourism Offices: Once you've arrived in a city, stop by the office. They can provide you with information about events, guided tours, and tourist destinations.

Hotel Concierge: If you're staying at a hotel, the concierge may frequently suggest and coordinate guided tours or activities for you.

Online travel discussion boards: Sites like TripAdvisor and Lonely Planet's Thorn Tree forum may be useful sources for locating tour operators and guides that other travelers suggest based on their own experiences.

Read reviews, research the reputation of the tour provider, and be sure they offer the experience you're after before making a reservation. You may explore Sicily's culture, history, and natural beauty much more effectively with well-planned tours and skilled guides.

Maps and Navigation Tools

To confidently navigate Sicily, you must have accurate maps and navigational aids. Here are some tools and resources to aid with efficient island navigation:

Google Maps is a flexible program that offers accurate maps, directions, traffic updates in real-time, and information on public transit. Additionally, offline maps may be saved for usage when there is no internet connection.

Apple Maps is a well-known navigation program that is accessible on iOS devices.

Turn-by-turn instructions, traffic updates, and places of interest are all provided.

GPS Tools: If you prefer stand-alone navigation tools, think about utilizing a GPS tool made for driving or trekking. Without utilizing a smartphone, these gadgets offer precise navigation.

Map Apps for Hiking and Outdoor Activities: Apps like AllTrails, Komoot, and Maps 3D Pro offer precise trail maps, elevation profiles, and GPS tracking for outdoor activities like hiking.

Local Transit Apps: If you want to take public transit, see if your area's transportation providers have their own apps for finding out about timetables, routes, and ticket prices.

Paper Maps: In regions with spotty mobile reception, having a paper map of Sicily on hand might be a useful backup. Bookstores, tourism bureaus, and internet merchants all sell paper maps.

Renting a GPS with Your Rental Car: If you're renting a car, several car rental businesses provide GPS systems for an extra cost. This might be a practical choice, especially if you don't want to rely on the data on your phone.

Local Information Centers and Tourism Offices: In large cities, you may find local information centers and tourism offices where you can pick up maps, brochures, and directions.

Online map services: Sites like OpenStreetMap offer thorough, user-contributed maps that are helpful for planning and exploring.

Apps that measure the position of the sun and compass:

Apps that offer compass readings and information on the location of the sun might be useful for navigating when participating in outdoor activities.

Keep in mind to have a backup plan in case of technical difficulties or battery drain. Downloading offline maps and keeping a paper copy on hand are both wise decisions. To guarantee easy navigation when visiting Sicily, become familiar with the tools you plan to use before your trip.

CHAPTER 10: Packing list, money saving ideas and Italian local phrases.

PACKING LIST

If you're going to Sicily, you might want to pack:

Shorts, skirts, and t-shirts are appropriate for Sicily's Mediterranean environment; bring them along with you.

Swimsuits: Keep your swimwear handy so you can enjoy the stunning beaches.

Bring good walking shoes if you intend to see historic sites and cities.

Sun protection measures include sunscreen, sunglasses, and a hat to protect you from the blazing sun.

Adapter: A gadget to charge your electronic devices with power.

Medication: Any required prescription drugs as well as standard first aid equipment.

Reusable Water bottle: Hydrate while cutting down on plastic waste.

trip papers: a passport, a government-issued photo ID, trip insurance, airline tickets, and any reservations.

Cards and Cash: A combination of local money and credit/debit cards.

Maps and a guidebook are useful tools for navigating the area.

Use your camera to record the breathtaking scenery and historical landmarks.

In particular, if you want to spend time outside, insect repellent is recommended.

Evenings can turn chilly, especially close to the seaside. A light jacket or sweater is recommended.

Beach towels are useful for picnics and days at the beach.

Handy for bringing groceries or souvenirs is a reusable bag.

Personal toiletries include toothbrushes, toothpaste, and other supplies for personal hygiene.

Keep your electronics fueled up with chargers.

Any Special Items: If you require any specialized items, such as trekking or swimming gear.

Keep in mind to adjust your packing list to your tastes and the activities you intend to engage in while visiting Sicily.

Budgeting techniques

Travel During Off-Peak Seasons: Going during the shoulder seasons (spring and fall) will enable you to save money on lodging and airfare while still taking advantage of the lovely weather and fewer crowds.

Alternatives for Lodging: Rather than booking a fancy hotel, think about staying in a hostel, guesthouse, or vacation rental.

Local Restaurants: Choose neighborhood trattorias, markets, and street food carts to sample genuine Sicilian cuisine at a fraction of the price of expensive eateries.

Cook Your Meals: If you have access to a kitchen in your lodging, acquire fresh ingredients from neighborhood stores and prepare some of your meals.

Enjoy Sicily's beaches, hiking trails, and public parks' natural beauty at no cost or no expense. On some days, a lot of historical places also provide free or discounted admission.

Rather than depending entirely on taxis or auto rentals, consider using public transportation to travel between cities and villages at a reasonable price.

City Passes: Determine whether the cities you are going to provide tourist passes that grant limited access to several sites and include public transit.

Cultural Events: Seek free or inexpensive cultural events, festivals, and concerts that may offer a distinctive experience without breaking the wallet.

Water and Snacks: To prevent making impulsive purchases in tourist zones, bring snacks and a reusable water bottle with you.

Group Tours: In certain cases, joining a group trip or tour is more affordable than planning a solo adventure.

Negotiate: If you're shopping at markets or tiny stores, don't be afraid to bargain a little to perhaps obtain a better offer.

A local perspective Find out where to dine, shop, and explore on a tight budget by asking the locals.

Cash withdrawals: Use ATMs to get cash in local currency instead of changing money at airports or exchange counters.

Plan and do your research: To benefit from offers and savings, research available activities, lodging, and transportation alternatives in advance.

Limitations on Souvenirs: Consider buying significant products that won't put a burden on your finances instead of spending too much on souvenirs.

To save money, keep in mind that your trip's quality need not be compromised. You may explore Sicily in awe-inspiring fashion on a budget with careful planning and wise decisions.

ITALIAN LOCAL PHRASES

1. Hello / Goodbye: Ciao (informal) / Arrivederci (formal)
2. Please: Per favore
3. Thank you: Grazie
4. You're welcome: Prego
5. Excuse me / Sorry: Scusa (informal) / Mi scusi (formal)
6. Yes: Sì
7. No: No
8. How much is this?: Quanto costa?
9. Where is...?: Dove si trova...?
10. Restroom / Bathroom: Bagno
11. Water: Acqua

12. Coffee: Caffè
13. Wine: Vino
14. Food: Cibo
15. I don't understand: Non capisco
16. Do you speak English?: Parli inglese?
17. Help!: Aiuto!
18. My name is...: Mi chiamo...
19. I need help: Ho bisogno di aiuto
20. Can you recommend a good restaurant?: Puoi consigliare un buon ristorante?
21. I'm lost: Sono perso/a
22. Can you take a photo for me?: Puoi fare una foto per me?
23. What time is it?: Che ora è?
24. I'm allergic to...: Sono allergico/a a...
25. I'm a tourist: Sono un turista.

Conclusion

To sum up, the Sicily Travel Guide 2023 serves as your ticket to a remarkable journey across this alluring Mediterranean jewel. Sicily provides an experience that is both educational and inspirational because of its long history, stunning scenery, and dynamic culture. Every turn unveils a new aspect of its distinctive beauty, from the busy markets to the peaceful coastal villages. You are prepared to explore the island's attractions, enjoy its culinary offerings, and relish its people after reading the insights in this guide. Sicily offers experiences that you won't soon forget, whether you're drawn to the archaeological wonders of Agrigento, the throbbing streets of Palermo, or the tranquil beaches of Taormina.

Remember to accept spontaneity as you set out on this voyage, make friends with the people, and savor every second. Your trip to Sicily in 2023 is calling, luring you in with the promise of exploration, adventure, and a tapestry of experiences that this island can only conjure. Pack your luggage, follow the tips in this guide, and see Sicily's enchantment come to life before you.

Printed in Great Britain
by Amazon